PATIENT TES

"I absolutely love Paschal Orthodontics' entire team. They made me feel like I've gained a whole new family! Highly recommend!"

—DEKISSIA JOHNSON

"We have loved our experience at Paschal Orthodontics. The staff is incredibly friendly, and my son now has a beautiful smile. They treat their patients with the utmost care and concern, and we could not be happier with this journey with them. Thank you to the entire team!"

—CHANDLER SCHOFIELD

"My son started treatment August 2017 and got his braces off April 16, 2019. The entire Paschal team was amazing from start to finish. We are thrilled with his new smile! My son said he can't stop looking in the mirror because his teeth are perfect now. That's a good feeling! If you are considering orthodontic treatment, run—don't walk—to Paschal Orthodontics. And trust me, I've used another practice in the area, and they don't even compare."

—DECHA MILLWOOD

"The office staff is so friendly, helpful, and knowledgeable. Dr. Paschal and his staff offer state-of-the-art technology while delivering the best customer service."

—MIRYN DAVIDSON

"As a patient of Paschal Orthodontics, I highly recommend Dr. Paschal if you or a family member need orthodontic care. Dr. Paschal and his staff's caring attention provide you with the feeling that you are the only patient. The friendly atmosphere in the office gives a relaxed experience at each appointment. I have complete confidence in Dr. Paschal and his excellent staff!"

—CAROL CASON

"If you are looking for a place that is family oriented, professional, and informational, this is where you want to be! Dr. Paschal and the team have become like family to my family! They have serviced two of my children, and my husband and I are looking forward to sending our youngest (if needed)."

—RANDEE SPENCER

"The Paschal Orthodonics team are the best! They provide a comfortable environment and friendly staff, and they are so attentive to your needs as a patient. They are truly a caring compassionate place of business and go the extra mile with their little extras!"

—TRACIE ELWER

"The staffs are beyond amazing. Absolutely love the fact that they all go to the extreme to make you feel welcomed and comfortable. Big thank you to Nicole for her top-notch service and having patience with me these last few appointments—so kind and sweet. Highly recommend this orthodontist."

—MARQUILLA LABORN

"Since day one, I have been more than satisfied with the whole team at Paschal. From routine appointments to last-minute struggles that come with an eleven-year-old boy with orthodontic work, they've always been able to help us super quick and are more than friendly. They keep parents informed but allow kids to be involved and feel 'grown' and special in the journey. We love Paschal Orthodontics! You won't find better."

—EMMALEIGH MOONEY

"We drive from Loganville, Georgia, for the great care we get with Dr. Paschal and his team. He is a very kind and outgoing orthodontist, and my girls love him. My pockets love him too. He is not quick to jump into unnecessary treatment to make more money off of you. We have completed one set of braces through his team and have three to follow, and we look forward to continuing to travel the forty-five minutes to use his practice."

—AMBER CARPENTER

"I lost my retainers several years ago, so as a result my teeth began to shift and become harder to clean. I also started not liking my smile because of the shifting. Paschal Orthodontics designed a liner plan that was easy to follow. The liners were so comfortable. The new apps and at-home scanning system helped me see my progress between office visits. I cannot believe that I am already finished with my treatment and about to start the retainer phase. Flossing and brushing are easier now. I am also so happy with my smile! The entire staff is amazing to work with! Thank you so much, Paschal Orthodontics!"

—JOANNE FRANTZ

"We couldn't be happier with our experience! Everyone is so friendly and professional. Madison is very fortunate to have Dr. Paschal! He is so knowledgeable, and his work is incredible!"

—DANA FLORENCE

"Took my granddaughter for her first appointment today. The staff was extremely friendly and welcoming. My grand-daughter is eight years old, and this is the first time she didn't cry and actually came out of her appointment smiling. That alone speaks volumes."

—DEBRA FRAZEE

"Dr. Paschal and his entire team are, hands down, the best medical team around! Giving someone their smile back is priceless, but they help me have a reason to smile just knowing I have been with people who truly care about me! I would recommend them to anyone in need or to those who just want to have more confidence in themselves. I love my results and will miss seeing these wonderful people so often!"

—JAN EMBRY

"From the very beginning of the experience, Dr. Paschal and his staff have been amazing. The office is like a well-oiled machine. Everyone is very friendly, communication is excellent, and even the office physical environment is pleasant. They remind you of appointments and there is very little waiting when you arrive. I can wholeheartedly recommend this office if you are in need of orthodontics."

—MELANIE COX

"We went today for our first consultation. We were blown away by the friendliness and expertise of their staff. Everyone was so welcoming, explained every step, and answered all our questions. We felt like part of the Paschal family from the moment we walked in. They used up-to-date technology to put a plan of action together that met our specific needs. My son who is typically uncomfortable in new surroundings felt comfortable throughout our visit. They are top notch and go above and beyond to make you feel welcomed and comfortable. We are excited to start our journey with them."

—JILL WADLEY

"Thank y'all for everything you've done for me! I never thought my teeth would be this straight. I appreciate it so much!"

—ASHLEY MILLIGAN

"You walk into the office and you are greeted with a smile. The waiting area was very comfortable and relaxing. The dentist and the staff in the office were amazing. My daughter was very nervous before the appointment, but they made her feel comfortable. Even though I was in the room with her, they spoke directly to her and answered all her concerns."

—KIMBERLEY PALMER

"Paschal Orthodontics has been nothing but amazing since we walked through the doors. They have worked miracles on my son's mouth. The staff is fabulous and very sweet. Now it's my turn!"

—TRILLAN CARTER

"This place is amazing! I'm probably one of their oldest patients. I had braces as a child, but my teeth started moving. I did Invisalign for thirteen months, and the result is great—no more gaps or spaces. The staff is awesome and they *always* greet you by name and make you feel welcome. I couldn't have asked for a better experience or results! Highly recommend!"

—KAY JONES

LIFE-TRANSFORMATIVE
SMILES

JAMES "JEP" PASCHAL, DMD, MS

LIFE-TRANSFORMATIVE
SMILES

ORTHODONTIC TREATMENTS AND TECHNOLOGIES
FOR THE SMILE YOU'VE ONLY IMAGINED

Published by Advantage, Charleston, South Carolina.
Member of Advantage Media Group.

ADVANTAGE is a registered trademark, and the Advantage colophon is a trademark of Advantage Media Group, Inc.

Printed in the United States of America.

10 9 8 7 6 5 4 3 2 1

ISBN: 978-1-64225-211-8
LCCN: 2022907280

Cover design by David Taylor.
Layout design by Mary Hamilton.

This publication is designed to provide accurate and authoritative information in regard to the subject matter covered. It is sold with the understanding that the publisher is not engaged in rendering legal, accounting, or other professional services. If legal advice or other expert assistance is required, the services of a competent professional person should be sought.

Advantage Media Group is proud to be a part of the Tree Neutral® program. Tree Neutral offsets the number of trees consumed in the production and printing of this book by taking proactive steps such as planting trees in direct proportion to the number of trees used to print books. To learn more about Tree Neutral, please visit **www.treeneutral.com**.

Advantage Media Group is a publisher of business, self-improvement, and professional development books and online learning. We help entrepreneurs, business leaders, and professionals share their Stories, Passion, and Knowledge to help others Learn & Grow. Do you have a manuscript or book idea that you would like us to consider for publishing? Please visit **advantagefamily.com**.

To Michelle: an amazing mother, business partner, and companion in life.

CONTENTS

FOREWORD

Finding healthcare professionals who have a breadth of clinical, research, and foundational knowledge, coupled with a "human touch," is becoming rarer as time goes on. Fortunately for you, the reader, you've found one of these individuals in Dr. Paschal. I say this confidently because I trained with Dr. Paschal and have enjoyed an enduring friendship with him for nearly two decades.

Dr. Paschal's unique educational and clinical background is genuinely that—unique. You would be hard-pressed to find an orthodontist that is also a trained prosthodontist, a dental specialist that focuses on only the most challenging dental/restorative cases. His experience as a prosthodontist is not only rare, it's valuable, and you will be the beneficiary. I was initially trained in a specialty quite different from orthodontics, which is why, I believe, Dr. Paschal and I became fast friends. We both shared the common ground of starting anew in a specialty we admired and were fascinated by, and lo these many years, we are still practicing orthodontists and very close friends.

This book is unique. It's not simply informative; it's personal. Dr. Paschal sincerely invites you to look behind the curtain and understand orthodontics and orthodontic treatment in *his* private practice. Almost every chapter and sub-chapter are introduced by relating the experiences of actual patients from Paschal Orthodontics. That's important because you are embarking on an adventure with Dr. Paschal and his team that will take time. In addition, you'll be a family member of his practice and know the experience as viewed by others who have been through treatment with Dr. Paschal and his office team.

You are fortunate to have found Dr. Paschal. He's a giant in the orthodontic world, widely known and respected by the best our profession offers. He's contributed, and continues to contribute, to the specialty of orthodontics, unlike most. And the best part? He and his team are genuine, beautiful people who love what they do and love the relationships they foster with their patients. I wish you well on your orthodontic adventure and want you to feel confident in choosing Dr. Paschal to walk with you through your experience. He's genuinely one of the very best.

—JOHN W. GRAHAM, DDS, MD
Salt Lake City, Utah

ACKNOWLEDGMENTS

When setting out to write this book about what we, at Paschal Orthodontics, do and what makes us different, I have to admit that it seemed almost impossible. What? Run a practice, manage a business, lecture, develop new ways of delivering care, be a father, and write a book? Are you kidding me? But as with everything in life, it takes a village.

My bride and partner in all aspects of my life, Michelle, deserves more thanks and gratitude than I could ever give her. Her guidance through our life together, being an incredible mother to our children, and prowess with both home and business finances make her the most important and impactful person in my life. It is safe to say that I could not do it without her. She makes me a better person and brings out the best in me every day.

There is no possible way to express my gratitude to the team at Paschal Orthodontics. These talented individuals make your experience unique and enjoyable. Without them, none of this would be possible. They direct me every day, and I love them for it. They make me a better orthodontist.

Most of all, I want to acknowledge you, the patient. Without you, none of this would be possible. Please know that your experience at Paschal Orthodontics is vitally important to us. I hope that the following pages help explain a few things about how we deliver orthodontic care at Paschal Orthodontics.

INTRODUCTION

Orthodontics is advancing at an amazing pace. New technologies are making the whole process of moving teeth faster, more comfortable, and more convenient. Although the biology of tooth movement has not changed, the methods that we now use to align teeth are much different from even five years ago. Today we rarely remove teeth, clunky headgear worn outside the mouth is a thing of the past, and we don't even have to use uncomfortable methods to expand the roof of the mouth. The treatments we use today are just so much more comfortable and convenient, and they make it much easier to meet the needs and schedules of our patients, almost half of whom are now adults looking for a more youthful smile—and a healthier bite. And now we can help you have that faster than ever before.

But as I said, orthodontics is about biology—something that is best left to the personal attention of trained professionals throughout treatment. Yet it can be very tempting to try out the do-it-yourself orthodontics that we've all seen on TV and the internet. These options make it appear that with only a few clicks we can have the smile we've longed for. That's simply not a reality for the vast majority. Here's what one of our patients, Jenny, had to say about making the choice to go with Paschal Orthodontics versus the online options:

> *My smile is very important to me—it defines me. I didn't have a serious issue with my teeth when I was younger. But as I got older, my teeth began to bunch up against each other, looking very uneven. Over time I found myself avoiding having photos taken. I was becoming so self-conscious, and that's not who I am. I'm someone who has a very public life. I'm on client calls and in meetings all day. So even though I really wanted to get back my smile, I really had no time and just didn't know how to make it happen. Finally, I decided to move forward and at least find out what my options were.*
>
> *I started by looking at some of the "do-it-yourself" internet options, but after reading about so many negative experiences and outcomes, I didn't want to go in that direction. I knew that there was one thing I did trust, and that was going to an orthodontist and knowing that I would have someone to reach out to for advice and consistent care throughout my treatment.*
>
> *When I found out that I could have orthodontic treatment with Paschal Clear—a custom, translucent, removable aligner, one that I could actually wear while doing business—I was so excited! It was so easy to get started, and the process was not at all painful. I've never looked back! It was one of the best decisions I've ever made!*

Even though orthodontic treatment happens faster than ever before, teeth do not move overnight. Again, moving teeth is a biological process, and there is much more involved in achieving a beautiful smile that also results in a healthy bite. It takes oversight by a trained and experienced orthodontist and team to guide treatment every step of the way. That's something you don't get with do-it-yourself options, also known as direct-to-consumer orthodontics. When patients need answers, they need someone to go to. But with so much misinformation online, it's difficult at best to get to the heart of the matter when it comes to options for having the smile and healthy mouth you've long desired.

I wrote this book to answer some of the questions that we get most often and also to share with you, the reader, why treatment at my practice, Paschal Orthodontics, is so special. It's so different, in fact, that our treatment is known as the Paschal Experience. Our relationship with you and your participation in treatment are central to everything we do here at Paschal Orthodontics.

Only a few years ago, most of our patients were children and adolescents. But now nearly half our patients are adults—and that number continues to grow. This book is for anyone considering orthodontic treatment at Paschal Orthodontics. It's for adults who are making an important decision for themselves or for their children. In the chapters ahead, I'm going to give you all the information you need to make that decision and also bring you up to date about state-of-the-art orthodontic treatment. After all, making the right decision is easier if you have all the information you need at your fingertips.

At Paschal Orthodontics we think differently about treatment in our practice. We know that orthodontic treatment is not just about the "today you" but also about the "future you" because the human body is not static. It continues to grow and change throughout your life. Your needs will continue to change, and the relationship between us doesn't cease at the end of today's treatment. We will be here for you long after your treatment is complete.

In the pages ahead, you will discover for yourself some life-changing stories that my team and I have been lucky to be a part of and the amazing technology that has made the movement of teeth so much quicker and more comfortable than it used to be. You will see how the Paschal Experience is about more than simply making attractive smiles; it's actually a step in helping people improve their lives.

CHAPTER ONE

THE PASCHAL EXPERIENCE

A great experience like no other!

When I came to Paschal Orthodontics for a complimentary consultation, I had known that I wanted to have my teeth straightened for a long time, but really didn't have any idea what to expect. I was excited, but also a bit worried....

The moment I walked in the door I was personally greeted by the treatment coordinator that I had spoken with when making the appointment. She was warm and welcoming, and we began a tour of the office, during which I found out a lot about how happy Paschal patients are when they finish their treatments. For many of them, it's really a first step in a new life. It reminded me of what I wanted to achieve—a transformation for my own smile. Never having to think about how my teeth looked when I opened my mouth to speak. Never again trying to hide my teeth when I laughed or even smiled. What a wonderful future to look forward to!

Now, months later, I have achieved that goal. It is such a boost to my self-esteem to know that now when I smile, I can do it with complete confidence. It was the easiest, most pleasant and comfortable experience I could have imagined, working with the Paschal team. What a difference this change has made to my life! But to be honest, I'm going to miss my regular visits to the office!

The experience you just read was shared by our patient Robin, and it's a familiar one shared by everyone who comes to Paschal Orthodontics for treatment. In fact, our offices have come to be known for what is called the Paschal Experience. It's why we have so many patient referrals from people who have already had their treatments with us and why our previous patients bring their children and other family members to us. Let me share a little more about what that experience is all about.

WELCOME TO THE FIRST STEP TOWARD YOUR NEW YOU

When you come to us for your first visit, you'll be greeted by one of our staff members, who will introduce you to your treatment coordinator. Your treatment coordinator will take you on a special welcome tour of the office, showing you around and introducing you to other members of our amazing team. We are a family-oriented group and pride ourselves on making our patients feel like they're a part of our Paschal family, and that begins with a warm welcome during the office tour.

When touring the office, it's common to notice the outstanding smiles of team members, many of whom were previously our patients and then came to work with us following their life-changing treatment. They are walking testimonials to the difference the Paschal

Experience makes.

On the tour of the office, you'll also learn about the amazing technology that we use for treatment. That includes intraoral scanning to make 3D digital renderings of your teeth (no more impressions or mouthfuls of choking goop) and 3D X-rays using cone-beam computed tomography (CBCT) imaging. These innovative technologies produce "digital impressions" of your teeth and mouth to help us get a full picture of your treatment needs. They are just some of the many innovative tools we will use to give you your life-changing smile.

In fact, the Paschal Experience is about using our skills and technologies to make your treatment as fast, convenient, and comfortable as possible. We even have technologies today that allow for remote office visits. With our system known as Paschal Remote, we can even monitor treatment without you having to come to the office.

For many patients the treatment itself is a combination of state-of-the-art appliances worn on the teeth for as few as four to eight months and then removing those and using clear aligners to finish everything off. Aligners, as you may know, are those transparent covers that fit snugly over the teeth to continue moving them into place. Today, in fact, almost all of our patients finish in clear aligners; and for about half, that's the sole type of treatment used for moving their teeth. Again, it's about comfort and convenience—whatever we can do to give you a beautiful, healthy smile in the fastest time with the fewest appointments possible. I'll talk more about the technologies and actual types of treatments used and some of the conditions that warrant the different options in the chapters ahead.

Affordability is also an important part of making treatment a memorable experience. At Paschal Orthodontics we know that treatment is an investment in your future, so we have custom payment options to make your orthodontic treatment an affordable decision for you and your family. I'll talk more about these options in the pages ahead.

Once we agree on your treatment plan, you will have the opportunity to begin treatment that same day. You've already invested time with us, so whenever possible, we like to make things as convenient as we can and take advantage of your time away from school or work.

Your excitement about the process is really crucial to a great outcome. We know that the best outcomes are those where the patient takes an active role in their treatment. Patients who take care of their teeth during treatment, follow the plan, keep us informed, keep appointments, and are excited about their future have the best outcomes. They know that orthodontic treatment is not just about who they are today but also about who they will be following treatment and in the years to come.

Patients who take care of their teeth during treatment, follow the plan, keep us informed, keep appointments, and are excited about their future have the best outcomes.

Your input also helps us customize your plan with the treatments, appointments, and timeline that fit your lifestyle—and your ultimate goals. Together, using our expertise and your input on your goals, we can come up with the best plan that works for you. Every patient is different, every situation is different, and that's why every treatment must be customized.

Just as your body continues to grow and change, so will your orthodontic needs, so our relationship is ongoing. It doesn't end when we remove the aligners; we'll be here for you long after your treatment is complete.

At Paschal Orthodontics, we want you to feel the difference and know that you're in the best place possible for your treatment. You can take comfort in knowing that there's someone walking with you every step of your treatment. We want you to be excited to see your progress week after week, and we want to share that excitement with you every step of the journey. We will be there as your new smile unfolds. That is what the Paschal Experience is all about.

Now let me take a moment of your time to share some background to help you understand a little more about *how* and *why* the Paschal Experience came about.

A LIFELONG INTEREST

One of the differences that make up the Paschal Experience is that I am one of the few orthodontists in the world who is trained in both orthodontics (a specialty in developing and moving the teeth and jaws) and prosthodontics (a specialty in restoring and replacing teeth). The unique combination of these two skill sets means we think differently about treatment at Paschal Orthodontics—it is more than just straightening teeth; it is about treatment that focuses on the overall health, look, and function of your teeth. We want your teeth to not only look straight and beautiful but also be in a mouth that is healthy and functions well.

Today in addition to treating patients, I am honored to be asked by my peers to speak to doctors, staff, and residents at international lectures and in orthodontic training programs on the most advanced orthodontic trends, techniques, and technologies that improve patient care. It's amazing to see the developments in the treatments that we're able to offer patients today—and those improve year after year.

As you can probably tell, I get pretty excited when I talk about orthodontics—in fact, I've been passionate about healthcare ever since I was a child. I was born in Columbia, South Carolina, but spent my childhood in Florida. As far back as elementary school, I had planned to work in the field of medicine. I loved keeping myself busy discovering new things whenever I visited a dental or medical office. At the dentist I was always inspecting the instruments, attempting to learn what each one was used for. The air/water syringe was a very cool *Star Wars* laser gun, and there were times when my dentist had to convince me that it wasn't a toy. But it still was to me.

Since my mother was a nurse for a pediatrician, I also gained a lot of interest in medicine early on that stayed with me through my high school and college years. During the school week while in elementary school, I would get off the bus and go to the office where my mom worked for the last few hours of her workday. The doctor was amazing with kids and often taught me things about medical lab work and X-ray machines—he let me see what kind of bacteria was grown in the lab and even let me take X-rays of my hands and feet. Needless to say, these interactions had a lasting impact on my curiosity about science and technology, and I'll always be grateful for the exposure because I know it took a lot of time and patience on his part to satisfy the curiosities of a child.

Later as a teenager, I had a close friend who had been born with a cleft lip and palate and had undergone many surgeries to correct the condition. As a teen he underwent orthodontic treatment, which back then wasn't nearly as advanced as it is today. For nearly six years, he wore braces and appliances to correct his teeth and bite, an extremely difficult and painful process that was compounded by taunting and teasing by the other kids. Brace Face, Metal Mouth, and Railroad Tracks were just a few of the nicknames he endured. While he tried not to show how much the teasing hurt, it ultimately seemed to define him during those growing years. He was shy and often uncertain around others, particularly girls, and it certainly affected his life in ways that even he could not define.

When his treatment was finally complete, he had a great smile, his mouth was healthy, and everything worked as it should. But watching him go through that process for so many years had an effect on me, and as a result, today at Paschal Orthodontics, we're very sensitive to what some kids face in school from their peers just because of their appearance. We know it's not easy for many kids, so if we can leverage a relatively new but well-tested technology to advance a patient's outcome in the shortest treatment time possible, we'll gravitate toward that.

When it came time to go to college, I steered away from dental school at the advice of my dentist, who believed the "golden age of dentistry" was over. Trusting his opinion, I began my undergraduate education at Emory University in Atlanta, Georgia, with the intent of becoming a medical doctor. I took all the standard premed classes—biology, chemistry, physics, etc. Then in my junior year, a friend of mine became ill and ended up in the hospital for an extended period. All that time in the hospital visiting her made me realize that, although I enjoyed medicine and really liked helping people, I didn't particularly enjoy the hospital environment.

I started looking for other options to change my direction, one of which was architecture, another area I have always been interested in—I always liked to draw and have a creative nature. Then the idea of dentistry came up again—interestingly it was one of the results in the many career aptitude tests I took at the time. So I started looking into dentistry and found that not only was the golden age not over but it also was a field ripe with potential. There were a lot of technological advances on the horizon. Plus, it would allow me to combine several interests at once: creativity, science, entrepreneurship, and helping people.

After dental school I did a residency in prosthodontics and then a hospital-based residency in general practice. During my year as a general practice resident, we did hospital rotations, and I learned so much about managing medically compromised patients that I believe it was possibly the best year of my education. That learning has been extremely valuable for our patients because it enables me to identify those with compromised health or when someone might need some extra measures before we begin treatment.

After completing those residencies, I spent five years working as a prosthodontist doing dental rehabilitations and implants. During this period I collaborated a good bit with a colleague who was an orthodontist. I would go to his office nearly every day and discover the incredible work he was doing; it was so interesting to learn so much more about orthodontics as an art and a science. Finally, at one point, seeing my excitement about the patients whom we worked on together, my colleague told me, "Jep, I think you're great at what you do, but I really think you should become an orthodontist."

Shortly thereafter I decided I would rather "move them than fix them," and my career path shifted toward orthodontics. I took his suggestion to heart, realizing that he was right. I wasn't meant to just make dental prosthetics to help people get by; I was meant to take what people had and make it better. So with my wife's blessing, we went back to school, and here we are today.

That's why, at our offices, it's more than just orthodontic treatment. It's more than making a beautiful smile. It's an experience— the Paschal Experience. We really see our role as helping patients take a few steps on their road to a better life. Using our experience and expertise, combined with technologies and caring, we really feel we are helping patients change their trajectory.

REMEMBER

- A key step in a great outcome is to choose the right orthodontic team.

- Your treatment should be customized to you and your lifestyle.

- Orthodontics is about the future you.

- Although internet treatments might seem like cheaper, quick-fix options for straightening teeth, it takes a qualified orthodontic professional and team—which includes you, the patient—to really have the best outcomes.

- We are there for you, side by side in this process, until you achieve the best outcome.

CHAPTER TWO

CHANGE YOUR TRAJECTORY

One day a young teen, Sherrie, came to my office with her mother. Sherrie was very shy and self-conscious—she hardly spoke a word during the consult and never looked anyone in the eye. Her shoulders were rolled forward, and she had long, dark hair that she almost literally wore over her face—as if it were a curtain she could hide behind and go through life unnoticed. She basically had all the diminutive traits of a wallflower.

Her problem? Extreme crowding in her teeth and very prominent canines (or fangs as they are sometimes cruelly called). In truth she was a very pretty girl, but her smile kept her from being her true self. As soon as she opened her mouth, her teeth distracted from her beauty. In fact, her mother told us that Sherrie was an excellent student but now no longer wanted to go to class—it was the start of a new school year in a new school, and Sherrie was being teased because of her teeth.

We began treatment that day, and over the next eighteen months, it was like watching a flower bloom. With every appointment Sherrie grew more confident and more outgoing. By the time her treatment was complete, she stood up straight, wore her hair back, and spoke easily with everyone she met, looking them straight in the eye. It was clear that she was becoming a confident young woman—it was the most glaring change I've seen out of all my patients. I have no doubt in my mind that the successes in her future will be in part because her parents chose to do orthodontics with us.

Sherrie is just one example of the transformation we often see in our patients. They come in ready to hide from the world and leave with a positive outlook on life—and on their futures. It is not an overstatement to say that having your teeth straightened is life changing in so many wonderful ways. We see it over and over again at Paschal Orthodontics.

Sherrie's story is not unique. Parents who want to give their child a better life often look to orthodontics as a first step in that journey. They know that giving their child a great smile can open doors to opportunities that they might not otherwise have because being able to smile at the world can instill confidence in every aspect of a person's life.

Imagine, if you will, your son or daughter learning to walk for the first time, learning to ride a bike, starting school, going to prom or graduation day, getting married, starting a career. Now imagine that same child with a beautiful, full smile—can you see your child's face at prom, at graduation, on their wedding day, shaking hands with a new boss? That's the difference that having straight teeth can make in your child's tomorrow.

IT'S ALL ABOUT PERCEPTION

Watching patients transform before our eyes is one of the reasons we love what we do at Paschal Orthodontics. Every patient who comes to see us has a special why for wanting treatment. Many are looking for a change in their life, but most don't have a real grasp on just how much their lives can change in ways that they have never dreamed of. Whether it's in their personal or business life, the sense of well-being and confidence that they gain from having straight teeth is a powerful, positive force.

But don't just take our word for it. Studies have shown that smiles actually make us feel better. A 2020 study, published during the COVID-19 pandemic (when smiles were harder to come by), found that just the act of smiling can improve your mood.[1] Studies have also shown that smiles are contagious both consciously and unconsciously.[2] When we see someone smile, it makes us want to smile, and that makes us feel happier. In other words a person with a big smile and positive outlook can change the tone of a room. Imagine if that were your child—or you. What kind of impact could that make throughout life?

Today in a world where a person's appearance makes all the difference, it's becoming more important than ever to have a great smile. The selfie generation has played a huge role in how people perceive one another, making first impressions all the more crucial. What better way to make a good first impression than with a great smile?

Beyond first impressions the appearance of a person's teeth can also make a big difference over the course of a lifetime. That's just one of the findings from a study on perception. Participants in the study were shown pictures of people—some with straight teeth, some with crooked teeth—and asked to give their opinions. Participants weren't told that the study was a comparison of the appearance of teeth, yet

---

1   F. Marmolejo-Ramos et al., "Your Face and Moves Seem Happier When I Smile: Facial Action Influences the Perception of Emotional Faces and Biological Motion Stimuli," *Experimental Psychology* 67, no. 1 (2020): 14–22, https://doi.org/10.1027/1618-3169/a000470.

2   S. G. Barsade, "The Ripple Effect: Emotional Contagion and Its Influence on Group Behavior," *Administrative Science Quarterly* 47, no. 4 (2002): 644–75, http://dx.doi.org/10.2307/3094912.

they viewed the people with straight teeth in a far more favorable light.[3] They saw them as happier, more loved, more successful, and even smarter. The majority of participants also said they felt they would be able to trust the people with straight teeth even more than they would trust someone wearing a nice outfit or driving a good car.

Perhaps it's no surprise, then, that the people with straight teeth were viewed as being more likely to get a job than someone with crooked teeth. That figure was confirmed by a study that involved submitting fake résumés with photos to a job application. The result? Attractive job applicants were five to eight times more likely to get a response by recruiters.[4]

What's more is that, when it comes to choosing someone on a dating site, those with straight teeth are seen as being more likely to get a date based on their photo alone.[5] In other words people with crooked teeth may be treated differently simply because they are perceived another way. That perception by others can then cause a person with crooked teeth to behave differently. They may be shy or avoid others. They may be bullied at school or even at work. They may be passed over for a job offer or a job promotion. Ultimately they may not smile as much or just stop smiling altogether.

In short, since teeth are the first aspect of someone's face that people notice and one of the features they remember most after they've met someone, beautiful, straight teeth simply imply a better

---

3   "People with Straight Teeth Considered Happier, Healthier and Smarter," *Dental Tribune International*, April 23, 2021, https://us.dental-tribune.com/news/people-with-straight-teeth-considered-happier-healthier-and-smarter/.

4   Rolf Bax, "Research: Attractive Applicant More Likely to Get a Job?," Resume.io, July 20, 2021, https://resume.io/blog/attractive-applicant-job.

5   "People with Straight Teeth."

life.[6] But there's even more going on than just perceptions. As we saw with Sherrie, a smile can actually change your whole demeanor.

A LIFE-CHANGING DIFFERENCE

When someone has confidence, it shows. It shows in the way they stand, the way they walk, the way they approach life. There's proof that a person's posture can affect their confidence. Standing tall, shoulders back, can actually help you overcome self-doubt, fears, and disappointments.[7] And a key to being confident is looking and feeling great about yourself.

The same goes for smiling. Happy people, it turns out, actually live longer. One reason is that all that smiling actually lowers stress levels—one study found that people who smiled while performing a stressful activity actually had lower heart rates afterward.[8] In fact, when you "put on a happy face," it can trigger mood-boosting chemicals in your brain.[9] So even if you're not having the best day, just smiling can actually make you happy. Those same chemicals help reduce pain and boost your immune system—literally making you healthier.[10] Even if your smile is not genuine, it can still improve your mood. But with a beautiful smile, there's no need to fake it.

---

6   Invisalign, "The 'Halo Effect': A Great Smile and the Road to Success," *Inc.*, October 10, 2017, https://www.inc.com/invisalign/the-halo-effect-a-great-smile-and-the-road-to-success.html.

7   Bryan Robinson, "New Study Shows Forming a Simple Smile Tricks Your Mind into a Positive Workday Mood," *Forbes*, August 13, 2020, https://www.forbes.com/sites/bryanrobinson/2020/08/13/new-study-shows-forming-a-simple-smile-tricks-your-mind-into-a-positive-workday-mood/?sh=3bd732252769.

8   "Grin and Bear It! Smiling Facilitates Stress Recovery," *Association for Psychological Science*, July 30, 2012, https://www.psychologicalscience.org/news/releases/smiling-facilitates-stress-recovery.html#.WNwlsZIWGi5.

9   Marmolejo-Ramos et al., "Your Face and Moves Seem Happier."

10   F. D'Acquisto et al., "Smile—It's in Your Blood!," *Biochemical Pharmacology* 91, no. 3 (2014): 287–92, https://doi.org/10.1016/j.bcp.2014.07.016.

You've probably heard that smiles themselves are contagious. Well, that's been proved too.[11] Your smile can make other people happy. When someone smiles at you, don't you want to smile back?

In short a beautiful smile creates change at both the emotional and physical levels—it can literally change the entire trajectory of someone's life. We here at Paschal Orthodontics are able to help the future you be better than anything you have ever imagined.

A NEW YOU AT ANY AGE

When Alice and her preteen son, Michael, came in for a consult, they both looked as though they had a secret and couldn't wait to tell me what it was. Alice started by saying, "My son is here to have braces. And—"

But before she could finish, Michael blurted out, "My mom is too."

After we all had a good laugh, he asked, "Can we both do it at the same time?"

I assured them that we could, and admittedly my team and I were as excited as they were about the two of them going through treatment together. Plus, it would be a family story for years to come.

After the consultation, which included 3D X-rays, I could see that Alice only needed minor correction that could be achieved with clear aligners, but Michael would be best served with a combination of traditional braces for a few months to correct his overbite, and then he would be able to finish treatment in clear aligners. Although Michael's friends at school were fascinated by his "grill," he really looked forward to wearing clear aligners so he and his mom could be in the same treatment at the same time.

Now that their treatments are finished, they love showing their

---

11   A. Wood et al., "Fashioning the Face: Sensorimotor Simulation Contributes to Facial Expression Recognition," *Trends in Cognitive Sciences* 20, no. 3 (2016): 227–40, https://doi.org/10.1016/j.tics.2015.12.010.

smiles together in photos taken at school events, family gatherings, and camping trips. Few parents get to experience having their teeth straightened at the same time as their children. But for Alice and Michael, it was great fun and helped create a bond they will share for a lifetime.

For many years Paschal Orthodontics primarily served children and adolescents. Today, however, adults make up nearly half of our patients—and that number is growing. There's a huge shift in the age range of our patients, and many of them are much older than you might think. To date I've actually treated several patients in their seventies and one woman in her eighties. It's never too late to invest in a new you.

REMEMBER

- The selfie generation has made a huge impact on everyone.

- First impressions can make all the difference in your personal and professional life.

- A smile can make you—and others—happier. It can also make you healthier.

- Treatment is no longer just for kids. Today many adults are having their teeth straightened as part of a new direction in life.

CHAPTER THREE

AN INVESTMENT IN YOU

Recently James came to see me about having his teeth aligned. It was something that he had always wanted to do, but he had put it off for years. What was stopping him? The cost. At least that was what he thought—until he was passed over for a promotion. "I always thought braces were expensive, but I didn't realize how much my crooked teeth were actually costing me," he told me during our consult.

It turned out that James and another salesperson where he worked were up for the same promotion to regional sales, a role that would come with a significant raise. They both had very similar experience, both had been with the company for the same number of years, and they were equals when it came to sales figures. But while James was friendly, outgoing, and a high performer—all the things needed in such a role—the other salesperson had a big smile full of bright, straight teeth. Ultimately James felt that was probably the deciding factor in why he was passed over for the role. It wasn't just about winning new accounts; it was also about having that winning smile.

We were able to correct his crooked teeth with a few months in braces, then finished off his treatment with clear aligners, which are difficult to detect on the teeth. In fact, James reported, once he was in clear aligners, that he had his best sales month ever. I like to think we had a small part in his achievement.

When it comes to braces, we see a lot of people hesitate to move forward with treatment because of the cost. We're seeing more adults these days because they have the means to pay for it, having achieved a higher level of career success, or because they are new empty nesters. But for children there's often hesitation from parents because the child's teeth seem to be working as intended. Although their teeth may not be straight, they are still able to eat a meal without difficulties, so orthodontics isn't seen as a priority.

But orthodontics is more than just straightening teeth; it's about instilling confidence and feelings of self-worth for a lifetime. Crooked teeth set you back, period. They set you back socially and emotionally; they keep you from feeling confident and ready to face the world. And with that comes missed job promotions (like James), networking opportunities, dates, or even spouse. It's rare that a person can overcome all that the world can bring on if they suffer from self-esteem issues and lack self-confidence due to crooked teeth. And everyone needs to be able the meet the world face-first. Having that edge as you go through life—something every parent wants for their child and for themselves—can pay back for the cost of orthodontics thousands of times over.

THE BEST INVESTMENT YOU CAN MAKE

One reason orthodontics is one of the best investments you can make is that treatment can last a lifetime. With orthodontics, once the teeth are straightened, the work is done. All it takes is some easy maintenance to keep your investment paying off.

To get the most out of your lifelong investment, however, it's best to have an experienced team guiding treatment. It might seem possible to achieve the beautiful smile you want with a mail-order company. But teeth are a living and changing part of you, and someone who has in-depth experience at working with moving teeth and is always attuned to changes in technology should be overseeing that movement.

With do-it-yourself or direct-to-consumer aligners, there may be some initial oversight to create the treatment plan, but once the aligners are created and mailed, the patient is solely responsible for treating themselves. Although the treatment plan is intended to be a road map, like any journey, things can happen along the way. Your teeth are unique to you, and they are going to move based on your unique circumstances. Moving teeth is a little like a tug-of-war game; we use existing teeth to put force on other teeth. So if a tooth doesn't move exactly as planned, it's important to have someone there to determine a change of course and ensure the journey ends at its intended destination. There are nuances to every movement, and it takes an experienced eye to know what it all means in order to guide every step of treatment. That's what we do at Paschal Orthodontics. We keep an eye on things to ensure the journey ends where it should.

Still, despite the lifelong outcomes that orthodontics can deliver, people often delay treatment—for years. There are any number of reasons why. One of the most common reasons we hear is that it's too inconvenient: there are too many appointments, it takes too long to complete treatment, and it's a hassle to take care of braces. We now have technologies that decrease the inconveniences of treatment. With clear aligners there are fewer appointments, treatment time is much shorter than ever before, and the aligners themselves are easy care. Yet we can achieve the same results. We even offer virtual orthodontics to reduce in-person appointments.

In fact, many patients want treatment in time for a special event or to fit around a holiday schedule. They may be okay with attending one family event, such as a Thanksgiving dinner, but they want treatment completed by the end of the year, when they meet with family for Christmas or other gatherings. With shorter treatment times, it's a lot easier to accomplish this for patients. Depending on when we start, we can often be done in time for the holidays or that special event.

A VALUE PROPOSITION TO CONSIDER

Let's look at it another way. What is the value proposition of an investment in straight teeth over time? What can it mean to your life? There's a way to explain this, and it involves a Volkswagen, of all things.

Back in the seventies and eighties, having braces or buying a Volkswagen cost pretty much the same—around $2,500. Back then braces literally took two full days just to be put on your teeth, and treatment time easily took two or more years. Yes, it could be very disruptive and time consuming.

The cost of orthodontics remains a fraction of what any automobile costs.

Fast-forward to today, and what does a new Volkswagen cost? Anywhere from $25,000 to $40,000—a 900 percent or better increase. In comparison the cost of orthodontics remains a fraction of what any automobile costs. A quality riding lawn mower costs more than the treatment we offer. Where I live in the South, you can buy braces for several members of the family for what a boat costs.

Here's the bottom line: for your investment, you're going to get a lifetime of use out of your smile. How often do you have to replace your lawn mower or your car? Yes, orthodontics is an investment—it's an investment in a smile. But that smile is going to make its wearer look and feel more confident. And that's going to open doors that you have never thought could open.

HOW DO I AFFORD IT?

For some patients this is one of the most important questions. "With everything else demanding a piece of my paycheck, how can I possibly pay for orthodontics?" At Paschal Orthodontics we are able to make treatment for yourself or your child affordable in many different ways.

For starters, thanks to technological advances, we can often do more with less. Nowadays, using clear aligners, we can often get the same outcomes for problems that used to require braces. We also offer several different levels of treatment, allowing us to tailor a plan that provides the best outcomes within your budget. The technological advances in orthodontics have also made it possible to restructure the fees in the practice, allowing us to offer payment options that are easier on the budget. Just like the treatment itself, we can customize payment options, including financing packages, to make treatment as affordable as you need it to be. We even have different levels of maintenance once treatment is complete, and we have an affordable prepaid maintenance program available that can provide a significant cost savings for taking care of your smile for the long term.

To start things off, we offer a free consultation to give you an idea of how we can help you have the smile you've longed for and how afford-able that can be. Our free consultation can clear up a lot of questions, including about costs—it's not uncommon for people to find out it's far more affordable than they think. Getting an answer to the question of affordability made all the difference to one of our adult patients.

Tanya came in for consultation in the wake of her divorce. She had always wanted to have her teeth aligned, but her former husband thought it was unnecessary. He always thought she looked fine, but Tanya felt like her crooked teeth were holding her back—in her career and in her social life. Even though it seemed they could always afford other things in life—nice cars, vacations, and other extras—orthodon-tics never seemed important enough to make it into the budget. Now that she was single again, Tanya had begun to move on with her life, and she wanted to look into her options for orthodontics. Since she was on her own and living within a new budget, making the treatment affordable was important to her.

When she first came in, she was somewhat reserved, but it was clear she was a woman who was beginning to find herself again, to put together a new life. She had a beautiful smile but a closed one—she had learned to smile without revealing her teeth, and it created a sense that she was holding back from showing her true self. She was at a point where she was considering entering the dating world again, so she was also looking for treatment that would fit within that new direction in life.

We were able to treat her with clear aligners and with a payment plan that worked out perfectly for her. Over the course of treatment, her personality began to change. She became more and more outgoing and talkative with my team and me. At one point she came into my office and was smiling broadly. "I have to tell you something really great that's happened, Dr. Paschal. I've just met someone, and I think it's moving along pretty quickly. I am so happy, but I never could have felt so confident about going out into the dating world again if I hadn't started treatment."

For Tanya, having teeth straightened with an affordable and convenient plan was an important part of picking up the pieces of her life and putting together a new one. Her situation was much like the treatment itself. It's often a matter of looking at the situation from the perspective of how we take what we have and make it all work together for an outcome that's both functional and beautiful.

REMEMBER

- A beautiful smile is the best investment you can make for yourself or your child.

- Today's technologies can make aligning teeth more convenient than ever.

- At Paschal Orthodontics we make it easy and affordable for you to have a beautiful smile.

CHAPTER FOUR

SOLVING THE PUZZLE—YOUR FUTURE SMILE

Simon came to see me about discomfort he was experiencing because of his misaligned bite. While talking with him, I could see the alignment of his teeth. I could see that he had already undergone orthodontics in the past, but the treatment had resulted in a "flat" smile. Rather than an upper row of teeth whose bottom edges naturally followed the curve of his lower lip when he smiled, the lower edges of his upper teeth presented in a straight line. That made his teeth appear artificial, like they were filed off flat—something that clearly had been caused by a human. Instead, teeth should have a natural-looking "scallop." They should be a little rounded where they meet tooth to tooth. The flatter the row of teeth appear, the older they make you look—it's a little like gears that have come together year after year and worn down. We may not consciously notice the difference, but our eyes certainly

LIFE-TRANSFORMATIVE SMILES

detect when teeth look unnatural. Simon knew it, and he wanted a change—that was why he came to see us.

More importantly I could see that his bite was not functioning well. His back teeth were wearing away at an increased rate. This would lead to more serious dental problems in the future. He started treatment that day, and we were able to give him not only a functional bite but also a more aesthetic smile.

We often talk about form versus function in orthodontics. While patients typically want to focus primarily on how their teeth look, my job also involves trying to get the best functioning bite, one that will help everything work well so that the patient can have a beautiful smile too.

> **I physically draw a line to show a relationship where aesthetics is on one end and function is on the other.**

It's rare that a patient is more concerned about function—they usually come to see us wanting an improved smile. In fact, only one patient comes to mind as being more concerned about function than appearance, and his case was fairly extreme. He was around seventy years old, was very active in sports, and had broken his jaw during a rock-climbing accident. His jaw had to be wired shut, and his bite was off as a result of the injury. We worked to restore that alignment so he could have a good bite again, one that was so comfortable and pain-free that it didn't remind him of the accident he had.

AESTHETICS — — — — — — — FUNCTION

Traditionally when I talk to patients about aesthetics and function, I physically draw a line to show a relationship where aesthetics is on one end and function is on the other. I often tell them that God doesn't care too much about aesthetics. God cares about your bite and the ability to chew since chewing is the first step in digestion. However, humans like pretty teeth and smiles. And my job is basically trying to get the best functioning bite to accompany the most beautiful smile.

THE MOUTH'S FUNCTION— IT'S A SYSTEM

The mouth is an amazing three-dimensional system where everything functions together to allow us to chew our food. Yet each tooth is an individual living part of you; each has its own function, and each interacts with another tooth in a harmonious way—similar to the way gears interact with one another. The teeth are individual pieces of ivory in arches that function against one another. During our younger years, each component—the teeth and jawbones—develop with the sole objective of giving each individual the best-functioning system to consume food and breathe. This doesn't always produce an aesthetic result. And even if the teeth do erupt and grow in two perfect rows, they are affected by strong forces over time.

Imagine a tree growing in a windy area. Based on the direction of the dominant wind, the tree may grow to lean a little due to the constant forces on it, whereas theoretically that same tree growing in an ideal environment, one void of the forces of wind, would grow straight up toward the sky. The teeth and jaws are no different; they also respond to their environment. Your teeth are located in what we call a biologic envelope, and they grow in an arrangement that is influenced by the forces that are delivered to them. Those forces include the jaws working together. Also, the tongue pushes out, and the cheeks push in. The teeth occupy the zone in between those forces. Simplistically speaking, teeth that appear crowded are indicative of too much force inward (the cheeks pushing in), and spacing between teeth means there is too much force pushing outward (the tongue pushing out).

One reason why it's so important to pay attention to function during orthodontic treatment is that the environment may not change. The tongue and cheeks are still going to apply force as well as the lips and chewing motions, and the teeth need to be able to respond to those forces. As an orthodontist it's my job to understand and compensate for the environment that those teeth experience. As we align your teeth, we monitor interactions that one tooth has with another in order to ensure the best outcome—one that functions well and looks great.

AESTHETICS—DESIGNING YOUR SMILE

Aesthetics in orthodontics is all about customizing the treatment plan to give you the beautiful smile that is best suited to you. While we start off with a smile design customized to you during treatment, as your teeth begin to move, we sometimes find that the goalposts move—the intended plan may need to change a bit. But my team and I will work to manage those moving goalposts before they become complications.

As I've mentioned we want to not only deliver great outcomes with your treatment today but also address your needs for the long term. When we've got a twelve-year-old undergoing treatment, we're not looking at his or her bite at age fifteen; we're trying to plan the bite and facial support that they're going to need when they're age forty-five. Yes, his or her teeth will wear and change over time, but treatment plans are not only intended for when a patient is young but they should also compensate for when a patient is much older.

We want to not only deliver great outcomes with your treatment today but also address your needs for the long term.

That's why I do not default to tooth extractions for many patients. Traditionally, orthodontic treatment has involved extracting teeth to alleviate crowding—that's the mechanically easy way out and can result in an unaesthetic outcome as the patient ages. Why? The soft tissue of a fourteen-year-old girl's lips and face are as youthful and supportive as they are ever going to be. Sorry, folks, that is biology. After age fourteen, it is all downhill. Think about a senior who wears dentures; when their dentures are not in their mouth, their lips sink in. If we were to remove four teeth in the back of a fourteen-year-old's mouth to resolve crowding, then at age forty-five or fifty, she won't have the facial support she needs for a beautiful smile—her smile will be narrow, and her lower face will appear more sunken in. In short, the decisions we make today can have a dramatic impact on the future. By striving to save teeth as a youth, there is a much greater chance that the patient as an adult will have a well-supported face and lips and have much more youthful facial aesthetics for longer. I talk more about orthodontics and the aging face in chapter 8. In the next chapter, I also talk about how the technologies we use today mean fewer extractions.

While treating to the future is crucial when performing ortho-dontics, one of my pet peeves is doing something out of fear for the future. Threats like "If you don't fix this today, you're going to have these fill-in-the-blank problems tomorrow" assume that one issue leads to bigger problems. That's not always the case. A lot of what you hear today has little, if any, science to back it up. But there are some causes—and likely consequences—of crooked teeth that can be expected. Let's look at a few.

CROOKED TEETH—CAUSES

There are a number of reasons why teeth become crooked in the first place. Here are a few of the more common ones:

- **Genetics.** By and large, one of the biggest factors in crooked teeth just comes down to genetics. If your mother or father has poorly aligned or crooked teeth, there's a good chance you will have them too.

- **Irregular eruption during development.** During devel-opment, early loss of baby teeth and irregular eruption of permanent teeth—teeth coming in out of place—can exacer-bate crowding issues.

- **Forces pushing in and out.** Earlier in the chapter, I mentioned how the muscular forces from the jaws, the tongue, and the cheeks all influence the environment where the teeth reside. Again, those forces from the jaws, cheeks, and tongue can alter the appearance of the teeth.

- **Poor hygiene.** Less-than-ideal teeth-cleaning habits, such as not flossing or cleaning teeth properly, can cause a cascade of problems in the mouth. Starting with cavities and potentially ending with deteriorated gum health, the lack of good hygiene can eventually lead to a less-than-ideal smile of crooked and even missing teeth.

- **Injury.** Teeth can be damaged by any kind of accident, whether from playing sports or a vehicle collision or simply falling down. If teeth are knocked out, shifted, or chipped after an accident, then other teeth may come in crooked or reposition to accommodate the changes in the mouth.

- **Poor nutrition.** Similar to poor hygiene, a poor diet can also play an important role in dental development for children and dental maintenance for adults. A lot of sugary soda and sweets in a daily diet can show up in the condition of a person's teeth.

CROOKED TEETH—CONSEQUENCES

Crooked teeth can lead to a number of problems in the mouth. A few that we commonly see include the following:

- **Less-than-ideal hygiene.** Simply put, straight teeth are easier to clean. When teeth don't fit together well, plaque can begin to build up in areas that are more difficult to tend to. Excess plaque (bacteria and debris) can damage or destroy the enamel, causing problems like cavities, temperature sensitivities, and soreness. In addition, poor oral hygiene (cleaning) can even lead to gum disease and, ultimately, tooth loss.

- **More wear, uneven wear.** When teeth are misaligned or do not fit well together, they don't function as well. That can lead to problems such as more-than-normal wear, uneven wear, and potentially even chips and breaks.

- **Difficulty chewing.** When teeth are crooked, missing, or causing pain, it can be difficult to eat some foods. That can lead to fewer choices when it comes to healthier eating. Foods that aren't chewed properly can also be more difficult to digest.

- **Underdevelopment of bone.** When crowded teeth are allowed to remain past adolescence, it can result in underdeveloped bone between the teeth long term. We see this quite often in adult crowded anterior (front) teeth, where the teeth overlap due to severe crowding. Although we can always straighten the teeth out, the bone between the teeth may never grow back after a certain age.

THE FOUNDATION—A KEY PART OF TREATMENT

Teeth can be moved even if they're not ideal, but sometimes conditions in the mouth mean visiting a dentist first to have a few foundational problems fixed; whether that's a cavity or periodontal disease, it needs to be treated before we begin orthodontics. My team and I will be happy to help you coordinate that treatment with your dentist and other providers.

Sometimes treatment also includes considering restorative work, such as crowns or bridges or even partial dentures or implants. Having a background in prosthodontics helps in identifying those problems and building solutions into the treatment plan. For instance, if there are multiple missing teeth, crowding, or teeth out of place because they've migrated into empty spaces where teeth were previously extracted, we will want to factor those foundational pieces into the treatment plan. It's all about getting puzzle pieces in the right places at the foundation to improve the final outcome—both functionally and aesthetically.

Not only do we design the bite and the smile to bring the aesthetics and the function together but another significant component of orthodontics is retention. Wearing a retainer after treatment helps the teeth resist the forces over time, reducing the need for extensive orthodontic treatment later in life or allowing for later corrections to be less intensive. I'll talk more about post-treatment retention and additional orthodontic corrections later in the book. For now let's delve a little deeper into how the teeth move and our very effective and efficient way of moving teeth during treatment.

REMEMBER

- Orthodontic treatment is about aesthetics and function, having a beautiful smile that also works well.

- Causes for crooked teeth include poor hygiene, injury, and poor nutrition.

- Consequences of crooked teeth include decay and pain, uneven wear, and difficulty chewing.

CHAPTER FIVE

SAGITTAL FIRST

Like most patients, Lisa came to see us to have her teeth straightened because, after seeing herself in photos online, she wanted a more attractive smile. She had beautiful, healthy teeth, but several of them were a little crooked, which ultimately took away from her smile and left her feeling self-conscious. After reading about some of the options available for straightening teeth and considering that only a few teeth were misaligned, Lisa thought that just a few months in clear aligners would give her the smile she desired.

But what she didn't know was that part of the reason her smile bothered her was that her jaws were not ideally aligned. Her upper teeth obscured her lower teeth more than what is ideal for a great smile because her lower jaw was set too far back in relation to her upper jaw. In treating Lisa we first addressed this front-to-back placement of the jaws and teeth using our Sagittal First approach, then we aligned her teeth with clear aligners to give her the radiant smile that she so desired.

Sagittal First is an innovative approach that has completely changed the way that we treat certain alignment issues and is the first step in how we change an irregular bite to a well-aligned one. Not only does Sagittal First result in much shorter treatment time but it's also much more comfortable for our patients. In addition, this approach can even reduce the need for surgical correction of jaw issues. Sagittal First works by taking advantage of the biology and architecture of the mouth.

> **Not only does Sagittal First result in much shorter treatment time but it's also much more comfortable for our patients.**

THE ARCHITECTURE OF THE MOUTH

Think about how the mouth is formed: there are two rows of teeth, one in the upper jaw and the other in the lower jaw, each shaped in an arch. The arch is one of the strongest features in architecture for supporting weight while allowing for objects to pass underneath. Sagittal First treatments use the strength of one of the arches to make significant movements in the opposing arch; by using one arch as an anchor, we can get the movement that's needed in the other arch to correct a bite.

In architecture the key to the arch's strength is the keystone or the uppermost section in the arch—the keystone distributes the weight throughout the structure. If you eliminate the keystone, the arch falls because it has no way to support the weight of the entire structure. Similarly in the arches of the mouth, the keystones (the front teeth) are crucial to getting movement. By removing them from the system and engaging only the sides of the arches—the posterior teeth—we're able to get the movement that we need in the sagittal plane.

The sagittal plane is one of three planes that orthodontic treatment focuses on. When it comes to the mouth and jaws, there are basically three different planes of movement: (1) the transverse or horizontal plane, which is what you see when looking at the head from the top; (2) the frontal or coronal plane, which divides the front of the head from the back of the head when looking at it from the front; and (3) the sagittal plane, which is the front-to-back relationship or how the jaws (and teeth) fit together when looking at the face from the side. With most patients the problems are transverse (side to side) or sagittal (front to back), and the vast majority of orthodontic treatments involve correcting these relationships.

For patients with transverse problems, orthodontic treatment typically starts with expanding the jaws side to side to make more room for all the teeth to be moved into place. In young children, that can be done with an expander, a device that is custom fitted and cemented to the upper teeth and roof of the mouth. It works well in children because there is a suture in the palate, or roof of the mouth, that does not fuse until late childhood; the expander allows the jaws to be widened to make more room for teeth to grow comfortably into the spaces they were designed to be in.

The problem with the expander is that it requires nightly homework—every night, Mom or Dad has to place a "key" into the expander in their child's mouth and crank it open. Not only is it a hassle for parents and children to go through that nightly ritual but the appliance itself also causes its wearer discomfort. Frankly expanders really aren't fun for anyone. Years ago I eliminated expanders in my practice by taking advantage of high-tech braces and advanced treatment approaches.

These days we've found it most effective to focus on the sagittal plane first—thus the treatment known as Sagittal First. We look at how the upper and lower jaws are related when viewed from the side of the head. From that viewpoint we can see whether the upper and lower jaws fit together as they should, and by correcting this plane first, we're able to handle a lot of the bigger movements first before finishing up treatment with braces or aligners.

With Sagittal First we use the teeth in one arch as an anchor to get movement in the opposing arch. We use what's known as Motion 3D appliance, invented by orthodontist Luis Carrière based on principles employed by his father, Jose (Pepe) Carrière. The appliance attaches to only two teeth on the upper and lower sides of the mouth, and then rubber bands are used to move the segments into a more favorable position.

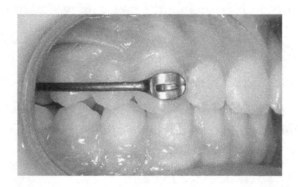

Class II

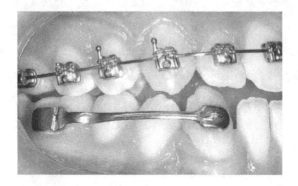

Class III

The result is movement that is more efficient—and faster. The motion appliance also vastly reduces the number of extractions that are necessary; as I've mentioned I try to avoid extractions for several reasons, one of which is the fact that it reduces the width of the smile. Because Sagittal First addresses some of the most difficult movements first, we're able to shorten treatment times considerably and reach our patients' goals faster. The motion appliance not only moves teeth into place but it also helps correct the front-to-back relationship between the two jaws.

For instance, with one type of correction, the upper back teeth move back as the lower jaw is pulled forward. A significant portion of the change occurs in what is known as the occlusal plane (or bite plane), which is essentially where the upper and lower teeth meet during a bite. Many sagittal treatments, such as headgear or what is known as the Herbst appliance, do not address this plane well, and it must be corrected with more force using braces after these treatments are removed.

The motion appliance allows more initial movement front to back and in the bite plane. Then depending on the amount of treatment remaining to move all of the front teeth into place for that beautiful smile, we use either braces or clear aligners—which I'll talk more about in the next chapter—to make the final alignments in the teeth. This technique has revolutionized our ability to use aligners in cases that we would never have considered using them in the past. While we're on the subject of moving teeth, let me share a little more about *how* teeth actually move and some of the classifications of teeth that help us determine movement.

THE MECHANICS OF MOVING TEETH

When it comes to moving teeth, I like to explain it as something like moving a fence post or mailbox pole through soft earth while keeping it perpendicular to the ground. If you were to simply push on the top of a post or pole, it would only tip in the direction that you wanted it to go, and the part underground would resist moving forward. To get the movement that you want, you must also apply a counterbalance. You must push or pull in a different direction somewhere else on the pole in order to get the entire pole to move through the ground.

Moving a tooth is the same: it's done by using slow and intentional forces applied at specific points on the tooth, which are determined by the placement of braces or by the design of clear aligners. That's where orthodontic experience matters; it's important to understand where to push on a tooth, how a tooth is likely going to move, and what's going to happen to other teeth as a result of that movement. What route is each tooth going to take as it moves into place, and what forces are required to get accurate movements during treatment? It literally is a three-dimensional puzzle that is solved by pushing and pulling between the individual pieces. Welcome to the world of orthodontics.

One of the ways we begin to make the determinations about where to push or pull is by looking at the basic construction of the mouth at the start of treatment. That is determined by what are known as classifications of bite patterns.

BITE CLASSIFICATIONS

There are three basic bite patterns that we address, and these are broken down into more classifications (most of which I won't detail here).

CLASS I—THE NORMAL BITE

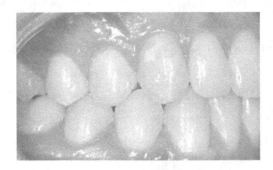

The bite patterns in this category are "normal," meaning the upper and lower teeth and jaws are creating a balanced bite. If this is what we see when you come into the office, then you will be moved into aligners or braces without Sagittal First treatment. A Class I bite is our ideal goal.

CLASS II—THE OVERJET (SOMETIMES CALLED AN OVERBITE BY PATIENTS)

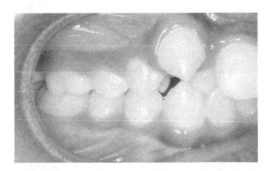

The majority of patients who have a discrepancy in need of treatment have what is known as a Class II bite. That means that the maxilla (upper jaw) and mandible (lower jaw) don't come together as they should. Looking at the person's face from a side view, either the upper teeth protrude farther than the lower teeth or vice versa. In some cases both rows of teeth protrude too far forward for the best function and aesthetics. When the upper teeth are too far forward, the bite is technically known as an *overjet*, although most people incorrectly refer to this as an *overbite*. (Technically an overbite is when the front teeth overlap too much when looking directly at them.)

With Sagittal First treatment, we can create the forces needed to move the teeth into the correct sagittal position. By attaching the appliance to the upper and lower teeth and then creating a connection between the two jaws with rubber bands, we can produce the forces needed to move everything into place—whether that means using the upper jaw as the anchor to help move the lower jaw backward or vice versa.

CLASS III—THE UNDERBITE

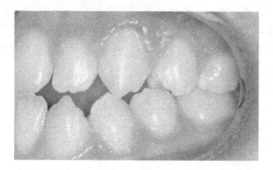

The beauty of the Motion 3D appliance is that we can also treat a Class III bite, also known as an underbite. This class of bite is when the lower teeth protrude farther forward than the front upper teeth, sometimes described as a "bulldog bite." To treat this bite, we bond the Motion 3D appliance to the lower posterior teeth (back teeth) and use rubber bands to pull the lower teeth and jaw backward.

Causes of underbite are often genetic in nature. If you have a close family member, such as a parent or grandparent, with an underbite, there is a greater chance that you will have this condition. It could also be due to an overdeveloped lower jaw or an underdeveloped upper jaw. With Sagittal First treatment, we can turn a Class III into a Class I bite.

OTHER BITE ISSUES

I've shared with you the technical classifications of the various bite patterns, but those are just the basics. We address many other problems with orthodontics, but some of the most common ones are as follows:

CROWDING

As I mentioned earlier, crowding is an issue caused largely by the force of the cheeks pushing in and from teeth erupting out of place. Crowding is the most common reason for crooked teeth. This is also the main reason for teeth to be extracted in many offices, resulting in a narrow smile, rather than a full, broad smile. Again, extractions are something we are often able to avoid these days due to the technologies we use. The technologies available today allow us to accommodate relatively severe crowding and create beautiful results.

SPACING

As mentioned earlier, spacing is another common problem we address with orthodontics. Like crowding, spacing is caused by the forces in the mouth. Spacing is usually caused by an imbalance of the force of the tongue pushing out.

CROSSBITE

Another bite problem that we commonly see is known as a crossbite, which typically affects only one or a few teeth in one area of the mouth. A crossbite is when a tooth or group of teeth do not line up correctly in relation to the tongue and cheek or lips when biting. For instance, upper teeth fit "inside" lower teeth when the mouth is closed or at rest. This malocclusion (bite discrepancy) can occur in both the back and front teeth, resulting in an anterior or posterior crossbite. A posterior crossbite occurs when the group of lower teeth toward the back of the mouth fit outside the teeth in the top jaw when biting down. An anterior crossbite occurs when the group of teeth in the bottom front of the mouth fit outside the teeth in the top jaw when biting down.

IN CLOSING...

With Sagittal First we can correct these and other bite problems first so that the jaws function well together and teeth come together well when biting down. It corrects the jaw at the beginning of treatment when there are no competing forces at work in the mouth caused by brackets or other appliances holding the entire arch as a single unit. Our goal with Sagittal First is to get teeth to the Class I platform so that we can subsequently move to braces or aligners.

Sagittal First usually takes no more than three to six months to reposition the jaws into a better relationship to each other while also helping improve the balance between the nose and chin. The treatment gently moves the bite into the proper position using light forces to move the teeth while maintaining healthy roots. When a treatment plan falls under the classification of Class II or III, treatment time can be reduced by one-half the conventional time by using the Sagittal First technique. Sagittal First can solve the most complex problems with ease and speed, moving the bite into a fully functioning position that is ready for further treatment.

The Motion 3D appliance is just one of the amazing advances in technology that are making treatment so much more comfortable, easier, and quicker. Let's look at some of the other technologies we use to treat patients today and compare some of them to how treatment was done in the past.

REMEMBER

- Sagittal First technology is making treatment time much shorter than in the past.

- Sagittal First takes advantage of the architecture of the mouth to make major movements.

- The Motion 3D appliance along with high-tech appliances allow us to achieve movements without tooth extractions or the use of uncomfortable expanders.

CHAPTER SIX

ORTHODONTICS— SIMPLIFIED

We were treating a young patient, Sara, when her mom told us about her own treatment as a youth. As is common with many such stories we hear from parents, that treatment included extracting teeth to make room for severe crowding in her mouth and wearing a type of appliance known as headgear, which is a clunky but effective way of straightening teeth. Parents today want their children to have beautiful smiles, but they don't want them to go through the same discomfort that they went through with their own orthodontics. They don't want their children to have teeth unnecessarily extracted, which later results in a narrow smile, and they

Advances in orthodontic treatment have significantly changed the way we move teeth— no headgear, no expanders, no parental homework.

don't want their children to have to wear clunky appliances during treatment.

Advances in orthodontic treatment have significantly changed the way we move teeth—no headgear, no expanders, no parental homework. The average treatment time for routine cases is ten to fourteen months. Some solutions can take as few as three to six months. And clear aligners often make it easy for people who are in the public eye to even avoid detection. Let's look at some of the treatments we use to move teeth comfortably, quickly, and easily and compare them with the old-school way of doing things.

EXTRACTIONS—ONLY WHEN NECESSARY

I've talked a bit about extractions previously, at least from the perspective of how much I prefer to avoid them, if possible. The problem with old-school technologies, some of which are still in use today, is that they did not always allow us to move teeth in the directions that we really wanted them to go. In order to compensate for the technologies of the past, extractions were often a necessary part of treatment—in some cases it was really the only way to make enough room to fit the teeth within the arches of the mouth.

Once the extractions were done, then braces were used to move teeth and needed to be periodically tightened by the orthodontist. We would remove the wires that went from tooth to tooth between the brackets, which were bonded to the teeth. Then we would tighten components of the braces and return the wires to the brackets.

But extractions result in narrow smiles; once teeth are removed, the face can be undersupported over time, and the lips and other facial features appear thinner rather than plump and full as the patient ages.

And in some cases, heavy force loads from braces would actually cause the roots of the teeth to resorb, or partially disappear, into the bone during treatment. Resorption weakens the stability of a tooth where it occurs. Years ago that was the only way to get the teeth to do what was needed to have a straight smile.

Fast-forward to today, and the braces we use have brackets that employ a technology known as passive self-ligation. I'll talk more about this technology a little later in the chapter. For now it's important to know that, in addition to the Motion 3D appliance that I mentioned in the previous chapter, the self-ligating system keeps us from having to do as many extractions as we once did. We no longer extract teeth due to crowding; we only pull teeth today if the orientation of the arches within the patient's skull requires it. Today that's maybe 1 to 2 percent of the patients whom we see. And the self-ligating braces employ even lighter forces, further decreasing the potential for negative consequences to the teeth and roots.

BITE CORRECTIONS—FASTER, MORE COMFORTABLE

In the past, bite corrections were often made with bulky and uncomfortable appliances, one of which I mentioned at the beginning of the chapter, known as headgear. Headgear is a device that attaches to the teeth but includes components worn outside the mouth that are attached to the head or face. It can consist of a head cap, fitting straps, a facebow (a metal U-shaped appliance attached to the molars that extends around the face and head), a chin cup, a forehead pad, and a mouth yoke. Some of the components must be removed while eating, though drinking through a straw is usually possible while the device is in. It is usually recommended for children whose jawbones are still growing, and it is designed only to correct a Class II bite, which is when the lower jaw is farther back than the upper jaw from the sagittal or side view. The device must be worn twelve to fourteen hours daily for as much as a year to correct the bite. And overall treatment can take as much as two to three and one-half years to complete.

Contact sports or play must be avoided while wearing because injuries can result from pressure against the headgear, and of course the gear can be damaged if mishandled. Children do not appreciate wearing headgear at school, as you can well imagine, and while most people wear the appliance overnight, it doesn't make for a great night's sleep. Headgear is still a very effective treatment and still in use today by some orthodontists. But it's not a comfortable treatment by any means, and we no longer use it at Paschal Orthodontics—there's no need because we have much more efficient, more comfortable options.

Another appliance that was used quite often to correct the bite—and is still in use today (although not at Paschal Orthodontics)—is the Herbst appliance, developed by Dr. Emil Herbst. Like headgear this appliance also corrects a Class II bite, which again is where the lower jaw is farther back than the upper jaw, causing the upper front teeth to stick out a little over the lower front teeth. The Herbst involves metal bands bonded to the back teeth, and then a rod is connected from the upper to lower bands. The appliance is left in the patient's mouth for about a year. It is bulky and often causes sores inside the cheeks. It also sometimes causes negative effects, which must be corrected with the braces later in treatment. All told, the treatment plan using a Herbst followed by braces can take two or three years. And if the appliance breaks, which it sometimes does during treatment, then the patient must be seen right away to have it addressed.

I actually used the Herbst appliance for many years to correct front-to-back alignment problems, until I found a far better treatment option in the Motion 3D appliance. As I mentioned in the last chapter, as part of our Sagittal First approach to treatment, this appliance allows for us to make the front-to-back correction far more efficiently and faster. Again, it works by using one arch as the anchor and removing the keystone or front teeth from the system by bonding the appliance to the posterior (back) teeth. The beauty of the Motion 3D appliance is that it can also fix Class III discrepancies, not just Class II. Plus, the time spent in the appliance is typically around four to six months, which is one-half or even one-third the time it takes for the Herbst appliance to complete treatment (not to mention the time in appliances after the Herbst appliance, which often increases due to the negative effects during the Herbst phase; again, that frequently results in overall treatment times of two and one-half to three years).

SELF-LIGATING BRACKETS

As I mentioned earlier in the chapter, today at Paschal Orthodontics, when braces are required in a treatment plan, we use an innovative type of bracket that employs what's known as passive self-ligation to move teeth. Passive self-ligation brackets use small spring-loaded doors to hold the archwire (the lightweight wire that moves the teeth) to the metal brackets. They allow for greater freedom of tooth movement and reduce the discomfort found in traditional braces. The nickel-titanium wire is custom-bent in the form of an arch, and because it has "memory," it is designed to move back to that arch form. That's how it methodically moves teeth into position at just the right pace and as determined by the treatment plan. It's a very low-force, low-friction yet very effective way to move teeth in the directions that we want them to go while maintaining proper bone and root health.

The brackets themselves are still available in metal, but they are also available in porcelain, which blends in with the teeth. Patients have a choice of using either type.

PALATE EXPANDERS— NO LONGER NEEDED

This orthodontic appliance creates more space in a child's mouth by widening the palate, or the roof of the mouth, to correctly align the upper teeth and jaw. It should only be used at a young age before the jaw is fully developed. Expanders are custom-made for each patient depending on the size of their palate and arch in the roof of their mouth.

I mentioned expanders previously as a method for widening the palate or roof of the mouth. To explain the technology a little more, the expander has bands that fit over a few back teeth in the upper jaw that are connected by a piece that spans the palate. That piece spanning the palate typically includes a screw that must be turned a little bit each day using a special key to create the tension necessary to expand the arch and widen the upper jaw, basically homework for the parents. It's a process that typically takes two months, but often the orthodontist will leave the appliance in the child's mouth for a few additional months to allow new bone to form in the expanded suture. As I mentioned, children have never been too fond of expanders nor have parents, who are tasked with the daily job of turning the screw and listening to their child complain about the pressure. Thanks to our high-tech braces, we no longer need to use palate expanders with our young patients, and we get great results in adult patients too.

X-RAYS—FROM ANALOG TO DIGITAL

As part of treatment planning, we want to get a good picture of the current conditions of the mouth. One way we do that is with X-rays. In the past we used analog X-rays, which provided a two-dimensional view of the teeth and gums and were the standard form of X-ray used. Analog X-rays provided us with good information, but it was somewhat limited because it took three-dimensional objects—the head and mouth—and turned them into a two-dimensional picture. Still, it was wonderful technology for its time.

Today we have the advantage of cone-beam computed tomography (CBCT), which provides us with three-dimensional views of the head and neck. CBCT is a specialized type of X-ray that provides much more information than conventional dental X-rays. It's a computerized, noninvasive scan that gives us a 3D look at hard tissues of the head and neck. The CBCT system rotates around you in approximately ten seconds using a cone-shaped X-ray beam with much lower radiation exposure than technologies of the past—less radiation than you are exposed to during a day at the beach. Using the digital images provided by a CBCT scan, along with the 3D model we obtain from our intraoral scanner (which I will explain next), we can get a full, three-dimensional view of the mouth—the teeth, the jaws, and even the bone structure below the tissues. That's enormous diagnostic power for creating the best smile design and treatment plan.

A great example of how the CBCT provides a far better view is something that I see routinely where teeth are trapped below the gums or tissues of the mouth and are not coming in properly—a situation known as impacted or "trapped" teeth. This occurs when there isn't enough room in the mouth for a new tooth to come in, so it stays partially or fully under the gums. Most commonly this happens with wisdom teeth but frequently occurs with other teeth as well. When teeth are impacted or trapped, I prefer not to remove them. Instead, it's better to try to save them, and we're able to do that with today's technologies.

With 2D analog X-rays, we could diagnose trapped or impacted teeth, but there was sometimes a need for additional X-rays to see exactly where the tooth was located and how it was coming in— and even then, there was sometimes a bit of educated guesswork involved. With the 3D view provided by the CBCT, I know exactly what's going on with every tooth in the mouth, even those impacted or trapped below the gums or hidden by tissue. That level of insight allows me to make a precise diagnosis and then bring in other professionals—such as an oral surgeon—if needed, to help with treatment. Depending on the situation, an oral surgeon can expose a severely impacted tooth and attach a "chain" to the tooth, and then we pull it into place using braces, thereby saving the tooth instead of extracting it.

INTRAORAL IMPRESSIONS—A NEW MODEL

As part of building the appliances needed for orthodontic treatment, we create a model of the mouth. In the past we made that model by filling the mouth up with impression material (known as "goop" by our patients), a soft, gooey substance that was (and sometimes still is) packed into a patient's mouth, allowed to firm up, and then removed. The physical model created by that process would then be sent to a laboratory, where it was used for diagnostic purposes or to create an appliance. In creating the appliance, the model was subsequently "lost" or destroyed and no longer usable. Today with digital impressions, it's no longer necessary to use this old-school way of creating a three-dimensional model of your teeth in dental stone.

With a 3D intraoral scanning device, we can create a digital 3D model of your teeth. The intraoral scanner is a wandlike device that allows us to take a series of about one thousand photos of every inch of your teeth and mouth. Together, those photos create a 3D rendering of your mouth, which we use to visualize your teeth and bite as we design your smile and create your treatment plan. Unlike the stone model, which is destroyed early in the treatment process, the digital model can be retained for as long as needed.

The digital scans increase our ability to customize the treatment plan for patients. With the digital scan on the computer, we have more capability to render a custom treatment plan for our patients and can even utilize it to visualize and finalize a customized plan for a specific patient's needs. It is a level of control that we never had in orthodontics until intraoral scanning technologies were invented. Having a clearer view of what to expect when a tooth moves is a far more effective way to treat patients.

Plus, the digital system allows us to shorten our clear aligner delivery times because, along with our in-house design software and 3D printers, we are able to do more of our own work in-house instead of outsourcing to a laboratory. These days our in-house digital scanner, design software, and 3D printers are key components of the Paschal Clear aligner system.

CLEAR ALIGNERS

For decades the only option available for straightening teeth was braces, those wire appliances that include brackets bonded to the teeth and then a wire threaded through the brackets that moves the teeth into place.

Then in the 1990s, a very bright engineer realized that if he did not wear his retainer nightly and his teeth shifted as a result, he could move them back into place by simply wearing his retainer again. Working with a software engineer and an orthodontist, the three created a system of clear aligners that, over time, have been refined to the point that we can now use the same type of product to do far more extensive treatment.

In fact, clear aligners are our most popular treatments to align teeth. They're orthodontic devices made of transparent plastic that are custom-formed to the shape of your teeth. They fit tightly over your teeth, and by progressively switching to the next aligner in a series, they slowly and gradually move your teeth into place. One of the great things about aligners is that, unlike braces, they can be easily removed during treatment for eating, brushing, or flossing.

Once we determine your treatment plan, then we create the necessary number of aligners needed to achieve your ideal outcome. That's the Paschal Clear aligner system. Our aligners are sent home with you to be switched out at prescribed points in treatment, typically weekly. We monitor the movements during treatment, and if changes are needed, then we can easily revise the treatment plan and create a new set of aligners because of our in-house capabilities.

Aligners are ideal for patients who don't want their appliances to show during treatment. Since clear aligners are removable and only worn for a specific number of hours each day, they are also a good choice for patients who don't want to deal with the food restrictions or special attention to cleaning that comes with wearing braces.

We also offer Paschal Refresh, which is a simple smile update using clear aligners. Paschal Refresh is ideal for patients who simply require a slight or small amount of movement to align their teeth. In the next chapter, I'll talk more about aligners and other treatments and how we decide which treatment will best fit your needs and lifestyle.

REMEMBER

- Today's technologies allow us to move teeth comfortably, quickly, and easily compared to the old-school way of doing things.

- Passive self-ligating brackets reduce the discomfort experienced with traditional braces.

- The Motion 3D appliance has replaced headgear and other front-to-back correction appliances.

- X-rays today provide a 3D view of the structures in the head and neck.

- Digital scans allow us to model the mouth without using goop.

- In-house technologies allow for far more control over the alignment process and allow us to shorten delivery times.

- Although advancing technologies are wonderful, the doctor you choose matters. Think of da Vinci; anyone could use the same paint and brushes he used to create his art, but he was a master, and through his artwork, it showed.

CHAPTER SEVEN

TREATMENTS TO FIT YOUR LIFESTYLE

I remember coming to my aunt's house for Thanksgiving dinner a few years ago. I had just gotten my braces. I knew, though, that would be the last Thanksgiving that my family would see me in braces. And at the Thanksgiving dinner celebration the following year, my relatives—amazed that my braces had already been removed—couldn't stop commenting on how beautiful my smile was and how it transformed me.

Dana shared this story with us about her experience with braces. For her, as it is with many of our patients, one of the primary concerns was just how long her treatment would last. Before innovations in technology changed orthodontics forever, braces typically had to be worn for eighteen to thirty months: two Christmases, two Hanukkahs, two family reunions, two Thanksgivings, and so on. But now the average treatment time for routine cases is only ten to fourteen months. That's because treatment at Paschal Orthodontics often involves a blend of various devices and modalities, designed around a plan to satisfy the patient's physical and emotional needs.

CUSTOMIZED TREATMENT PLANS

In previous chapters I talked about how we first fix the front-to-back bite relationship in patients, as well as the various appliances we use during treatment, depending on the need. To recap, when designing a patient's smile, the first thing we look at is whether they need a motion appliance to fix their front-to-back bite, or the sagittal plane. If they do need a motion appliance, then pending any foundational work, that appliance is the first step of treatment (see chapter 5, "Sagittal First," for more information).

Where treatment then differs is with what follows the front-to-back alignment of the bite. Once the bite is aligned, then we look at whether their smile can be finished off with clear aligners. If not, then we know that they need to be in braces—using high-tech, self-ligating brackets—for a certain amount of time.

Typically, however, even complicated cases transition to braces for six to nine months and then finish in clear aligners. For instance, if a patient's bite is fine and they do not need a motion appliance as a first step of treatment, but they have a severe crossbite, then those kinds of corrections are better managed with braces. This kind of treatment might require being in braces for seven to twelve months and then moving into clear aligners for the remaining months of treatment.

Think of it this way. The braces do the heavy lifting if necessary for more complicated issues. Once these foundational concerns have been addressed, we can move into aligners for the final months of the treatment.

For various reasons, some patients actually prefer braces over clear aligners, and they may stay in braces until treatment is complete. They may want them simply for the prestige of having orthodontics, or they may want them because, depending on the person's lifestyle, braces may actually be easier for them to care for than clear aligners. If braces are required (or desired) for treatment, then our technologies allow us to move forward with treatment the same day.

If a patient doesn't need a motion appliance to fix their bite as the first step, then we look at whether their treatment can be done with aligners. Again, depending on the complexity of the case, we may be able to do the full treatment with clear aligners—no need to consider braces for any portion of the treatment. If aligners will do the job, then we've got the technologies in-house (the Paschal Clear system) to move forward with their treatment that day.

In short, treatment today is basically about mixing and matching appliances to specifically meet each patient's needs at specific times during treatment. By using clear aligners for a portion or, in some cases, all of the treatment, we can significantly shorten the amount of time it takes to straighten teeth. That's something that really concerns most patients. Like Dana at the beginning of the chapter, patients don't mind showing up for a holiday meal in braces once, but they don't want it to happen two years in a row. Thanks to another innovation, we can even reduce the number of in-person appointments for many patients.

VIRTUAL TREATMENT

Virtual treatment is an exciting development that is having a significant impact on orthodontics. There are certain stages of treatment where it is simply not necessary to come in for an appointment, so we make it easy and convenient to see us for a consultation from the comfort and safety of your own home. Through our program known as Paschal Remote, we can monitor your treatment without you having to come in for periodic appointments. Paschal Remote combines virtual evaluations, machine learning, and patented algorithms in order to create a self-administered remote monitoring system for orthodontic care. It is designed to work with most treatment plans and allows you to basically send a "selfie" of your teeth so that we can monitor the progress of your treatment.

Virtual monitoring involves downloading an app to your preferred smartphone device and attaching a device to your phone's camera to "scan" your mouth to provide us with an update on how treatment is progressing. All you have to do is follow the instructions to take your own scans and send them in, and then we can see precise tooth movement, tooth health, how well you're brushing, whether any elastics are being worn properly, and so much more. All this can help lead to faster treatment times and less frequent visits. With virtual monitoring, patients are able to take more responsibility for their treatment, something that can actually help accelerate the timeline.

YOU CAN INFLUENCE YOUR OUTCOMES

Whether it's elastics, aligners, or the care a person takes with their teeth (brushing, flossing, eating the right foods), treatment outcomes depend largely on compliance by the patient—both children and adults. Dana, whose story I mentioned at the beginning of the chapter, started off her treatment with a question asked by the majority of our patients: how long before my braces can come off? While my team and I are here to help you through every step of treatment, the answer to that question depends, in part, on the patient's participation.

When you come in for your first visit, we will give you an estimate of treatment time. This will be based on our evaluation of how complex your orthodontic issue is and the expected response of your teeth to the plan we create. But it's important for you to also realize the role you have in your outcome. You, as the patient, have a lot of influence on how quickly your treatment can be completed. If you do your part at home with keeping your teeth clean and gums healthy, your treatment can go as quickly as the biology of your teeth will allow. We've seen it over and over again—better tooth and gum health actually helps teeth move faster. There are fewer problems with cavities and gum recession to delay treatment, and good oral health just makes for a far better outcome all around. By being an active participant in your treatment, following our recommendations and instructions, you can actually help shorten the amount of time you will spend in braces.

The bottom line is that once you choose to invest in orthodontic treatment, then we do all we can to encourage you to see that commitment through to the beautiful smile you've wanted for so long. Determining that level of commitment is one component of treatment planning. We really want to know just how much time and effort you plan to put into your treatment to help us determine, for instance, whether braces or aligners are the best choice. Let me explain.

By being an active participant in your treatment, following our recommendations and instructions, you can actually help shorten the amount of time you will spend in braces.

Some years ago my sister-in-law—who had a great sense of humor—came in for orthodontics. I noticed early on that her treatment was going a little slower than I had expected it to. But the mystery was solved when I asked her whether she was wearing her aligners. She laughed about it, saying, "I don't understand why these aligners aren't working. They are with me in my purse all the time."

It's easy enough to understand: treatment that involves aligners or other removable components, such as rubber bands, only works if those components are in place in the patient's mouth as planned. With aligners it's easy to take the appliance out to eat and then forget to put it back in right away after brushing and flossing. Aligners have to be switched out at certain points during treatment for everything to move as planned; if they don't get switched, then treatment may not go exactly as planned. Aligners are also easy to forget about when, for instance, eating out—we've fielded many calls by patients who removed their aligner and placed it in a napkin, only to toss out the napkin with the rest of the trash at the end of a dine-out meal. (We have procedures and technologies to help deal with such accidents.)

For these reasons and others, aligner treatment may not go at the pace we plan, but small incidences like these do not completely derail treatment. Yet these kinds of incidences are why we try to have a better understanding of the patient's lifestyle when creating the treatment plan. Knowing how you—or your child—live your life can give us a realistic idea of how you (or your child) will comply with instructions.

For example, if the patient is an adult who has a daily exercise regimen, sticks to a strict diet, and always seems to be on time, then he or she will probably have the discipline and commitment to do very well with aligners. On the other hand, an adult who has an extremely busy and changing schedule and must always be reminded of appointments may find that they prefer to wear braces rather than add the responsibilities that come with aligner treatment to their day. If it's a child who is really good at wearing contact lenses, doing homework without being told, or brushing their teeth regularly without prodding, then they're probably going to do a good job of keeping their aligner trays in or wearing their rubber bands. But if it's a child who struggles to keep track of their glasses, can never seem to locate their homework (much less complete it on time), and must constantly be reminded to brush and floss their teeth, then odds are their treatment is going to require a little more parental involvement.

Whatever the treatment, our goal is to satisfy both the physical and emotional needs of the patient. We want to ensure we're using the right appliances and creating the best treatment plan, but that plan needs to also take into consideration how to make the patient feel and perform as a member of the team. That's the bottom line: it takes a team to have the best outcomes, and the patient—and sometimes the parent—is a key member of that team. We don't just put on braces or give you a set of aligners and send you on your way. We're going to be with you every step of the way.

REMEMBER

- Technology has greatly reduced treatment time.

- The average treatment time for many cases is only ten to fourteen months.

- We use a range of treatments that are customized to your lifestyle.

CHAPTER EIGHT

WE'RE BY YOUR SIDE IN THIS LIFE PROCESS

When I first came to Paschal Orthodontics for a consultation, I thought that Dr. Paschal would probably have to pull some of my teeth. I had teeth that were sitting up high on my gums, higher than my regular teeth, and couldn't imagine what else he would do with them. But to my surprise, he told me that he did not want to pull any teeth. He wanted to keep them and move them down to be part of what he called my "best natural smile." He told me that if he were to pull those teeth, that would affect the full width of my smile. He also explained to me that as we get older, it's best to keep all of our teeth because that will give us the necessary foundation for our overlying lip support.

I remembered seeing my mother from the side and noting how thin and almost sunken in her lips appeared, and then I connected a memory that she had four teeth removed when she had braces as a kid. Suddenly I completely understood what Dr. Paschal meant about needing to keep a good foundation for the future. It made me feel so good to know that he was looking out for my long-term well-being in this process in a way that I couldn't have even imagined before we discussed it.

Because our bodies are constantly changing, our teeth are as well. Treatment is not finite: gravity sucks down and forward. This is something I tell my patients all the time, and they often respond with "Don't I know it." We see changes in our bodies and faces as we age. Ten years from now, any plastic surgery—such as a face-lift—will look different from what it did when the treatment was first completed. Teeth are no different; they keep functioning, wearing, moving, and changing. They also have to accommodate facial growth and changes. There are many influencing variables, and teeth can shift as a result.

Of course, we all need to embrace the aging process. But this fact doesn't mean that you can't be better prepared for it and ensure that you look and feel as good as you can. When it comes to orthodontics to address the aging face, the Paschal team is on your side. We're a partner in this life process that you're trying to improve.

THE AGING FACE

We see a lot of patients that have had straight teeth throughout their lives. But when they come in, they tell us, "You know, I don't understand why I'm here because I've already done this once." That "done" was orthodontic treatment, and that "once" was actually twenty years earlier. Or maybe they never had braces when they were a kid, but now as they're getting older, their teeth are getting more and more crowded. All of that is part of the normal aging process.

Your body isn't the same as it was twenty years ago. There's absolutely no reason to think that your teeth are going to be the same. Teeth shift because of our human physiology. Even someone who faithfully wears a retainer for fifteen years following earlier treatment still experiences some minor shifting of their teeth.

At the same time, the gum tissue, lips, and cheeks get thinner with age. They don't retain their resiliency over time. The collagen (the framework of your skin) gets more bound up and less supple. And because of this, the tissue becomes thinner and can't stretch like it used to. This, in combination with normal bite wear and slight jaw growth, comes together as a complex combination of forces, which results in more crowding of the teeth as we get older.

A YOUTHFUL SMILE CAN MAKE ALL THE DIFFERENCE

The smile is actually the foundation of facial aesthetics; a beautiful smile makes you want to smile more and can even make you look more youthful and vibrant. As discussed in chapter 2, too often we see that people embarrassed by their teeth ultimately train themselves not to smile as broadly as they can. That can actually have an impact on you and the people around you. Most people also want to look younger for longer, and there's nothing wrong with that. A beautiful smile makes all the difference by giving a more youthful appearance and showing a personality that is perceived as open and friendly.

At our office we see this positive impact over and over again. We see that children who aren't proud of their smile come in with a more diminutive, less responsive facial expression, even during full laughter. They have learned to consciously pull their smile back. Unfortunately this behavior works its way into the sub-conscious, which is why it's best to take care of a child's teeth as early as possible to avoid any negative effects on their personal and emotional development.

The American Association of Orthodontists recommends that all children have an orthodontic evaluation by the age of seven. Children often do not need treatment until around the age of ten to thirteen, but if there are serious issues, some problems are more easily treated at a younger age.

> *We love the family-centered practice at Paschal Orthodontics. Both our children came here, and although at first they were a little afraid to have dental work done, they completely forgot their worries when they came into such a friendly environment. The staff took the time to make them feel comfortable, and the children loved going there. We just had family portraits done, and they were gorgeous. Thank you, Dr. Paschal and your great team, for everything you do.*

For children and adults, being able to show your smile, to be able to show joy, surprise, or happiness without being self-conscious about it, is a significant part of your well-being. Regardless of whether you've had orthodontic treatment in the past or not, wanting properly aligned teeth is not about appearing vain; it's simply about wanting a better life. And a beautiful smile can make all the difference.

IT'S NOT A FACE-LIFT BUT KIND OF

Maintaining a youthful smile comes down to having a strong underlying foundation for the soft tissue facial structure. To achieve a fuller smile, as people get older, they often look to having injectables put into their lips. However, the reality is that your teeth are the foundation that supports your lips and the tissues of your lower face. If your teeth and jaws are not well aligned and in the best position, injections may make lips and the surrounding tissues look plumper and more youthful, but ultimately they will not have the support they need to keep that appearance. Ensuring good underlying structure can come from a good orthodontic treatment plan, one that brings everything into alignment.

As I said at the start of this chapter, gravity sucks down and forward. The "down" part of that process is what causes the face to appear thin and drawn. The "forward" part is the jaw growth, bite wear, and resultant crowding. For example, at my age my lip is almost covering all my upper teeth. When I was younger, it only covered half of my upper teeth. You have probably noticed that older people actually start showing more lower teeth. That happens because as we get older, our lower lip hangs down a bit more. The lips are a bit like a curtain. As we age, that opening sags more and more. This happens because the collagen starts to get thinner, and tissue and muscle tone decreases. It's an unavoidable process.

Years ago I remember an orthodontist telling me about how his staff had begun to notice something interesting about their patients. When they would align the teeth of those who were forty-five and older, the staff could see that, at the end of the treatment, the skin tissue covering the lower part of the face always showed a marked improvement in support. The reason for this is that the overlying tissue of the face now had a uniform foundation after the teeth were aligned, and as a result, facial creases and what are referred to as "marionette lines" were not as prominent. The staff actually started calling this procedure a "brace lift" because orthodontic treatment, although not designed to address facial sag, did just that.

Recently we began working with a patient who had already had injectables put in her lips as a way of trying to offset the effects of having had four teeth pulled when she was younger. In spite of the injectables, she still hated her smile, so she came to see what orthodontics could do to help her regain a more youthful look. She did not want braces, but during our discussion, I explained to her that although we could try to adjust her teeth with clear aligners, it would be much more effective to use braces to address the straightness she wanted to achieve and give the tissue around her upper jaw a firmer foundation.

We are also treating her young daughter and have opted not to pull any teeth because we know her daughter's future just by looking at the situation her mom is facing. As I've mentioned previously, we avoid extractions whenever possible because we don't want to debilitate your future smile by condemning it to an undersupported face. We also don't want to see your child go through life with a constricted, reduced smile instead of the big, broad, and beautiful smile that they could have had.

OPTIONS FOR MAINTAINING THE FUTURE YOU

At Paschal Orthodontics we look at smiles for the long term. We know that having your teeth straightened is more than a onetime process; it requires retention once the initial treatment is complete. That means once you have your beautiful smile, we want to help you keep it, so we send you home with a retainer that is to be worn as prescribed to keep your teeth straight.

Even then, over time as teeth shift and facial structures age, you may need a slight refresh of your smile. That's normal, and it's one reason we created various tiers of programs for maintaining your smile. The three programs we currently offer include the following:

Paschal Total. The Paschal Total program covers the traditional fees for full orthodontic treatment, including the retainer that you are to wear to keep your teeth straight. It is our most popular program.

Paschal Elite. The Paschal Elite program covers the traditional fees for full orthodontic treatment, including an initial retainer, along with an aftercare program. That aftercare program includes a discount on replacement retainers. Paschal Elite also includes a program at a substantial discount for Paschal Orthodontics patients who later need an update to their smile. Typically these are patients who had orthodontic treatment earlier but, over time, experienced some shifting of teeth because they didn't wear their retainers or because of the natural forces of aging. The update usually involves using a number of clear aligners to restraighten the teeth and bring back a more youthful smile.

Paschal Refresh. The Paschal Refresh program is for patients whose teeth only need a little adjustment to bring them into alignment. Currently it includes limited treatment using fewer than twenty clear aligners simply to straighten teeth.

All of our programs are available with low down payments and low monthly payments. These days we're even able to offer a payment schedule that extends beyond the initial treatment. Our goal is to make it as easy and comfortable as possible for children and adults to have the smile they desire for a lifetime.

REMEMBER

- Because our bodies are constantly changing, our teeth are as well.

- Even with a retention regimen, age-related crowding can affect teeth over time.

- To keep a full broad smile, we don't pull teeth. We prefer to reposition them.

- We are here to support you through all the changes your teeth may undergo.

- We strive to make orthodontic care affordable for your personal financial needs.

CONCLUSION

I had been asked so many times to write a book about orthodontics that I finally decided to do it. Yet with two busy practice locations and lots of great patients to see, admittedly it was a challenge at first. Yet once I started, the words flowed easily, and I found that I really enjoyed sharing the information on each page. I looked forward to sharing these insights with you, the reader, to help answer the questions that we get every day at Paschal Orthodontics.

My team and I love to be amazed by patients with the stories of how their lives have changed. We love working at a place where we get to see the transformations that happen to patients during and after their treatment. It is enormously rewarding to all of us here at Paschal Orthodontics to see not only teeth move into place to create beautiful smiles but also what those smiles do for patients' lives. The difference it makes in so many people's lives is one of the reasons we love what we do.

Investing in orthodontics is an investment in not only your appearance but also your health and well-being. It's an investment in your self-confidence that will have a huge impact on your life or your child's. A beautiful, healthy smile is more valuable than ever before—whether you are seven or seventy. It is the starting point of giving a positive first impression wherever you go.

Although orthodontic innovations will continue to evolve, I have tried to give you as much current information as possible. I wanted to include as much as I could about all the important things you need to consider when choosing the right professional who will take the best care of you or your family. Today's technologies and cutting-edge treatments and innovations move teeth more effectively and efficiently than ever before. From diagnosis during the initial consultation to various types of treatment and update options years down the road, I hope that I've shared with you enough information to see what it's like to pursue treatment for the smile you've long desired.

We've also looked at a number of stories from our patients that illustrate some common situations, one or more of which may be similar to your own and can help give you some insight. As you by now know, social media has had a huge impact on our concepts of aesthetics and beauty—not always in a positive way. But with orthodontics, not only can you and your family members see the change in the mirror (or in a selfie) but you can also experience the upbeat way that you approach the world once you have that beaming smile.

I thank you for indulging me while sharing my professional background and how I came to be an orthodontist. I think this gives my team and me a significant edge when it comes to the quality of treatment you and your family members will receive. One of the most important things you need to consider when choosing an orthodontist is the background of the provider. Remember that lower cost often equates to lower quality, and that can also mean much longer treatment time as well as additional office visits and fees.

When you become a patient of our practice, you are more than just someone with teeth and jaws that need attention; you are someone we get to know and help over the course of your life. I hope you see, by sharing some of our own stories, how easy it is to get to know us—and how much we want to know you. Here at Paschal Orthodontics, we are on your side throughout the life process to help you be your best. We're part of a process that is not simply a one-off. We're here for you down the road.

At Paschal Orthodontics, quality and your comfort are the most important considerations when designing a smile for you that is both functional and aesthetic. That's why we don't believe that mail-order or do-it-yourself alignment is a better option, especially if you are looking for top results and follow-up care that will determine the quality of your smile for the rest of your life. Again, at Paschal Orthodontics, the relationships we build with our patients and their families are of utmost importance to us. Our referrals tell the story about what we proudly refer to as the Paschal Experience. We know that we can achieve the best results for you and your family—it's what we do every day, and we love doing it for you.

We are looking forward to seeing you soon in our offices for a consultation. We'll show you exactly how we can help you achieve that beautiful smile that you have always wanted. And we look forward to seeing how, as with all of our highly satisfied patients, your new smile will transform your life.

ABOUT THE AUTHOR

Dr. Jep Paschal is a proud husband, father of three, orthodontist, technologist, and orthodontic futurist. He has had the privilege of lecturing all over the world helping orthodontists learn the value of digital orthodontics, in-office aligner design and manufacturing, the Sagittal First treatment philosophy, and the passive self-ligation treatment philosophy. He received his BS from Emory University and his DMD from the Medical College of Georgia. He also completed residencies in prosthodontics and general practice and earned his master of science degree in biomaterials and prosthodontics at the University of Texas Health Science Center at San Antonio. Dr. Paschal maintained a private practice in prosthodontics and implant dentistry before returning for a residency in orthodontics at the University of Rochester Eastman Dental Center.

Dr. Paschal has served on the board of directors for the American Association of Orthodontists Foundation, as president of the Georgia Association of Orthodontists, as a member and chairman of the Council on Communications for the AAO, and as a member and co-chair for the AAO Future Think Tank. Dr. Paschal currently maintains a private orthodontic practice in Madison and Lake Oconee, Georgia, USA. His hobbies include family, computers and technology, reading, skiing, and travel.

CPSIA information can be obtained
at www.ICGtesting.com
Printed in the USA
JSHW020819210622
27321JS00002B/58

9 781642 252118